A

P

Welsh and English

Compiled by Tegwyn Jones
Illustrated by Brian Fitzgerald

Appletree Press

First published in 1996 by
The Appletree Press Ltd
19-21 Alfred Street
Belfast BT2 8DL

Printed in the UAE.

A Little Book of Welsh Proverbs

A catalogue record for this book is available from the British Library.

ISBN 0 86281 624 6

9 8 7 6 5 4 3 2 1

Introduction

Proverbs crystallise the most common of human judgements and experiences. As a result, the same proverb can occur in many different languages, since the essentials of human needs remain the same across the globe.

But each different society gives its proverbs a tincture of their own. This is very true of Celtic society, with its emphasis on honour, hospitality, courage, and its taste for the poetic. These Gaelic proverbs, like little geological cores raised up from far-buried strata, give us a set of insights into a society now gone. It was a rural society of farmers and hunters, with time to fight as well as time to make verses. Its wealth was counted in cows and corn rather than in cash. Gaelic proverbs reflect this closeness to nature and an attachment to the rhythm of the year. The short, ironic comment, often intended as a delicate put-down or a reminder of human fallibility, is dear to the Celtic mind, and from such a base, proverbs emerge quite naturally, and with distinctive wit and pithiness.

And, though that Celtic society is long gone, its proverbs remain and still, perhaps, give a special insight into the minds of their descendants. They are part of what makes us what we are.

Gormod o bwdin a dagith gi.

A surfeit of pudding will choke a dog.

Cynt cwymp dâr na miaren.

Sooner will an oak tree fall than a briar.

Gwell bachgen call na brenin ffôl.

Better a wise lad than a foolish king.

Heb ei fai, heb ei eni.

He who is blameless is not yet born.

Y cyntaf i'r felin gaiff falu.

The first to the mill will be the first to grind.

Chwery mab noeth, ni chwery mab newynog.

A naked lad will play, a starving lad will not.

Gorau prinder, prinder geiriau.

The best economy, economy of words.

Gochel y pechod cyntaf,
canys y mae lleng yn dynn wrth ei sawdl.

Beware of the first sin,
for there are a legion hard on its heels.

Ceffyl da yw ewyllys.

Determination is a good horse.

Yr oen yn dysgu'r ddafad i bori.

The lamb teaches the ewe to graze.

Derfydd dannedd merch yn gynt
na'i thafod.

A girl's teeth will wear out sooner than her tongue.

Dyfal donc a dyrr y garreg.

A constant knock will break the stone.

Gellir diddanheddu'r blaidd ond ni ellir ei ddinaturio.

A wolf's teeth may be removed but not his nature.

Taro'r post i'r pared gael clywed.

To strike the post so that the partition hears.

Gall pechod mawr ddyfod trwy ddrws bychan.

A great sin can enter by a small door.

Canu cyn borefwyd, crio cyn swper.

To sing before breakfast is to weep before supper.

Ci yn udo noson ole,
newydd drwg ddaw yn y bore.

A baying dog on a moonlit night;
mournful news in the morning bright.

Gwell swllt da na sofren ddrwg.

Better a good shilling than a dud sovereign.

Gŵr heb bwyll, llong heb angor.

A man without prudence is a ship without an anchor.

Lle bo eglwys gan Dduw bydd capel gan y diafol.

Where God has a church the devil will have a chapel.

Gŵr dieithr yw yfory.

Tomorrow is a stranger.

Tyfid maban, ni thyf ei gadachan.

An infant will grow,
but his swaddling clothes will not.

Allwedd arian a egyr pob clo.

Money is the key that opens all locks.

A ddywedo leiaf, hwnnw yw'r callaf.

Who speaks the least, he is the wisest.

Pan fo llawer yn llywio fe sudda'r llong.

When the steersmen are many the ship will sink.

Na ad i'th dafod dorri'th wddf.

Let not your tongue cut your throat.

Gorau cam, cam cyntaf.

The best step, the first step.

Er heddwch nac er rhyfel,
gwenynen farw ni chasgl fêl.

Not in war nor in peace will a dead bee gather honey.

Da yw Duw a hir yw byth.

God is good and eternity is long.

Gelyn i ddyn yw ei dda.

A man's wealth is his enemy.

Segurdod yw clod y cledd.

A sword's honour is its idleness.

Gwin yn y bol, twrw yn y pen.

Wine in the belly, tumult in the head.

Eilfam yw modryb dda.

A good aunt is a second mother.

Gwell aros o alltudedd nac aros o fedd.

Better a waiting from exile than a waiting from the grave.

Gwna dda dros ddrwg, uffern ni'th ddwg.

Repay evil with good, and hell will not claim you.

Hir y byddir yn cnoi tamaid chwerw.

A bitter morsel will be chewed for a long time.

Hawdd cynnau tân ar hen aelwyd.

It is easy to kindle a fire on a familiar hearth.

Haw dywedyd "mynydd" na myned drosto.

It is easier to say "mountain" than to climb one.

Digon yw ychydig yn fwy nag sydd gennyt.

Enough is a little more than you already have.

A elo yn hwch i Rydychen,
yn hwch y daw yn ôl.

A sow that goes to Oxford will still be a sow
when she returns.

Hir y bydd y mud wrth borth y byddar.

The mute will tarry long at the gate of the deaf.

❦

Cynt y cwrdd dau ddyn na dau fynydd.

Sooner will two men meet than two moutains.

❦

Cyfaill blaidd, bugail diog.

A wolf's friend, an idle shepherd.

Blys merch yn ei llygaid,
blys bachgen yn ei galon.

A girl's lust in her eyes,
a boy's lust in his heart.

Addo teg a wna ynfyd yn llawen.

Fair promises will make a fool happy.

Nesaf i'r eglwys, pellaf o baradwys.

Nearest to the church, furthest from paradise.

Pe gwisgid coron am ben pob ffôl,
ni a fyddem bawb yn frenhinoedd.

If a crown were to be placed on every fool's head,
we would all be kings.

A fynno glod bid farw.

He who desires to be praised, let him die.

Amynedd yw mam pob doethineb.

Patience is the mother of all wisdom.

Bedd awen gwely priodas.

The marriage bed is the grave of the muse.

Cam dros y trothwy, hanner y daith.

A step over the threshold is half the journey.

A heuo ddrain, na fid droednoeth.

He who sows thorns, let him not go barefooted.

Call gŵr a ddyco ei elyn yn gâr iddo.

Wise is the man who makes a friend of his enemy.

Cwsg gwir ar ddrain, ni chwsg anwir ar blu.

Truth will sleep on thorns,
lies will not sleep on feathers.

Ennyn cannwyll i chwilio am haul canolddydd.

Lighting a candle to search for the midday sun.

Yr euog a ffy heb ei erlid.

The guilty one will flee without being pursued.

Chwynnwch eich gardd eich hun yn gyntaf.

Weed your own garden first.

Dywed yn dda am dy gyfaill;
am dy elyn na ddywed ddim.

Speak well of your friend;
of your enemy say nothing.

Ni ddaw cof i chwegr ei bod yn waudd.

The mother-in-law forgets that she was a daughter-in-law.

Doeth ffôl tra tawo.

The fool is wise while he remains silent.

Ni chwyn yr iâr fod y gwalch yn glaf.

The hen does not complain because the hawk is sick.

Hy pob ceiliog ar ei domen.

Every cock is bold on his own dung heap.

Digrif gan bob aderyn ei lais ei hun.

Every bird delights in his own voice.

❦

Nid twyll twyllo twyllwr.

It is no deceit to deceive a deceiver.

❦

Heb wraig heb ymryson.

Without wife without strife.

Y neb a anwyd i rot nid eiff byth i bum ceiniog.

Whoever is born to fourpence will never achieve fivepence.

Y mae dafad ddu ym mhob praidd.

Every flock has its black sheep.

Y mae dau du i bob tudalen.

There are two sides to every page.

Ffordd yr â ci ydd â'i gynffon.

As the dog goes so goes his tail.

Cyd bo hirddydd, daw ucher.

Though the day be long, evening will come.

Y cyw a fegir yn uffern, yn uffern y myn drigo.

The bird reared in hell, there he will choose to dwell.

Angel pen ffordd, diawl pen pentan.

An angel on the highway, a devil at home.

Câr dy gymydog ond cadw dy glawdd.

Love your neighbour but maintain your hedge.

Dau drwg dalu – talu 'mlaen a pheidio â thalu.

Two bad payments – to pay beforehand
and not to pay at all.

Cwsg galar ond ni chwsg gofid.

Grief will sleep but anxiety will not.

*Melysaf y cân eos, ond nid erchis
Duw i'r frân dewi.*

Sweetest sings the nightingale,
but God did not command the crow to be silent.

"Tin du!", meddai'r frân wrth yr wylan.

"Black arse!" said the crow to the seagull.

Glew a fydd llew hyd yn llwyd.

A lion will be valiant to the end.

Ni wna'r llygoden ei nyth yn llosgwrn y gath.

A mouse does not build its nest in the cat's tail.

Deuparth gwaith ei ddechrau.

A job started is two parts done.

Nid yn y bore mae canmol diwrnod teg.

The morning is not the time to praise a fine day.

Gwell asyn a'm dyco na march a'm tawlo.

Better an ass that bears me than a stallion
that throws me.

Utgorn angau yw peswch sych.

A dry cough is death's trumpet.

Gan y gwirion ceir y gwir.

One gets the truth from the simple.

Godrir buwch o'i phen.

A cow is milked from its head.

Gair i gall, ffon i'r anghall.

A word to the wise, a stick to the unwise.

Henaint ni ddaw ei hunan.

Old age comes not alone.

Mae hen gof gan hen gi.

An old dog has an old memory.

Ymryson â doeth, ti fyddi ddoethach.

Contend with the wise, you will be the wiser.

Na sang ar droed ci chwerw.

Tread not on an angry dog's foot.

Ni waeth beth fo lliw'r delyn os da'r gainc.

It matters not what the colour of the harp is
if the melody is sweet.

Lle crafa'r iâr y piga'r cyw.

Where the hen scrapes the chick pecks.

Gwell cariad y ci na'i gas.

Better a dog's love than his hatred.

A ŵyr leiaf a ddwed fwyaf.

He who knows least talks most.

Anodd tynnu cast o hen geffyl.

It is difficult to cure an old horse of a bad habit.

Canmol dy wlad a thrig ynddi.

Praise your country and live in it.

Unwaith yn ddyn, dwywaith yn blentyn.

Once a man, twice a child.

Buan ar farch, buan i'r arch.

Swift on his horse, swift to his coffin.

Ofer cadw ci a chyfarth fy hunan.

It is futile to keep a dog and do the barking yourself.

Mae tân yn gyfaill da ond yn elyn drwg.

Fire is a good friend but a bad enemy.

Aeth y newydd ar gyrn a phibau.

The news spread on horns and pipes.

Cân di bennill mwyn i'th nain,
fe gân dy nain i tithau.

Sing your grandmother a sweet song,
and she will sing to you.

Dianc rhag y mwg a syrthio i'r tân.

To escape from the smoke and fall into the fire.

A wnelir liw nos a welir liw dydd.

What is done by night will be seen by day.